THE DOLL HOUSE

THE DOLL HOUSE

LITTLE TINY VISIONS

Edited by

GENIE CHIPPS HENDERSON

with
Priscilla Bowden Potter & Sheridan Sansegundo

Photographs by

RAMESHWAR DAS

Design by

MIKI DENHOF

THE PUSHCART PRESS

With special thanks to Joanna Rose
for her generous support of LTV,
to our founders Frances Ann and Frazer Dougherty,
and to all the friends and members of LTV
who lent their talents to this project.

CONTENTS

HOME AGAIN

We're smaller by the minute: yesterday
still grownups, an hour ago teens,
then kids for a while, and now
we're in our blue pajamas, here
at the top of the stairs, holding
pink rabbits, all ears.
The walls shrink down to our size,
the banister on the landing
so short now we can see over it tiptoe
into the yellow lamplight where
Mommy and Daddy are playing house, their voices
drifting upstairs, not words
but lullabies—the murmurs make us drowsy,
and as he comforts her and lies down
beside her on the couch, we lose
our grip on furry rabbits, and drift away
to grass and summer sunshine, hardly knowing
when they rise from the couch and creep upstairs
and carry us like dolls
back to bed.

Philip Appleman

The Doll House exterior measures 36" x 24" and is 36" high. The scale is one inch to one foot. There are fourteen rooms on three floors. The faded stucco has been purposely distressed with cracks and weather stains to signify the wear of many decades.

The Doll House interior is illuminated in a blaze of light from chandeliers, sconces, lamps, even the single bare bulb in the attic.

In this miniature medium fine-tuned craftsmanship teams up with illusion and whimsy. The stained glass panels on either side of the front door repeat the Liberty pattern of the wall covering in the entrance hall. The stained glass windows in the upstairs conservatory are copied from the title page of *A Book of Verse,* written & illuminated by William Morris.

scale: one inch to one foot

A FOREWORD

Do real people live in this house? Is a real artist about to lay his brush on the canvas in his studio, has the maid just stepped away from her ironing, is the lady of house, having left her half eaten peach on a plate in the dining room, on her way up the hall stairs to her writing desk where work on a novel appears to be going badly?

As a real house, it might have been built in the late 18th century but we are looking at it in 1924. It is the kind of house that is easily found in the English or Irish countryside. A country house, comfortable but not grand, lived in by its more modern heirs.

Here in the country, there are plenty of servants to keep things running smoothly while Papa paints and Mama writes and everyone takes tea and reads. The genteel occupants appear to be devoted to art and literature, parties and lawn games and all manner of up-to-date and sophisticated pastimes. A Brancusi resides in the conservatory, Sonia Delaunay, Modigliani, Matisse and Mondrian hang on the walls. Oscar Wilde muses from the study and on the bookshelves are the works of Virginia Woolf and E.M. Forster. The curio cabinet holds fossils found on the beaches of Lyme Regis; in the nursery there are exotic toys from grandfather's missionary days in China. And who was it sent that crate from Cairo? Never mind, it all found a home in the Egyptian dining room.

Who has created this miniature fantasy world . . . and why?

Both the doll house and the book result from a collaboration among a band of writers, artists and crafts people residing at the tip of Long Island,

12

New York. Those of us who make this place our home call it the East End. Others—the media for example—and most everyone from elsewhere, refer to this stretch of beach and the small villages and towns hugging the Atlantic Ocean some 100 miles from New York as the Hamptons—fabled resort of the very rich, the very celebrated, the very chic.

It can take as much as four hours to drive that modern horror, the Long Island Expressway, from New York City to the Shinnecock Canal, but having done so the highway will narrow to local roads surrounded by ocean, bays and inlets. Between the famous resorts of Southampton, Bridgehampton and East Hampton are open fields and farmland where row upon row of potato plants run to the white dunes and the sea. The East End is divided into two forks—the more rural North Fork of wineries and farmstands and the South Fork aka the Hamptons. But the notion of the Hamptons really only exists in the gridlock of summer lemming time when it often seems we select each day a different traffic jam in which to spend some time.

Fortunately, the rest of the year, after those who visit and play have returned to the smart watering holes of autumn, we who live here settle down to a more quiet life. Then, almost surreptitiously, pleasure boats head into dry-dock, the surf breaks on a deserted Amagansett beach, storefronts glow in the deep blue of a November sky, parking can be had and the towns and roads are reclaimed by pick-up trucks and the ever attendant black Lab dog riding shotgun. The East End has come back again.

East Enders are about as various and varied a group as you are likely to find anywhere. We are an artists and writers colony, a place of famous names and interesting people who started coming here more than a century ago. At the turn of the century, William Merritt Chase and Childe Hassam began the great art migration to the East End. Artists claim there is a particular light here unique because we are surrounded by water. Jackson Pollock lived, drank, painted famously, died and was buried here, proving that excessive drinking, anxiety about work and four fast wheels make a terrible cocktail. Jimmy Ernst worked here as did Fairfield Porter and Elaine de Kooning. Larry Rivers lives here and so does Willem de Kooning.

The writers started coming in the '30s. The more they came, the more they stayed, finding the sea and relative peace entirely to their taste. John Steinbeck lived in Sag Harbor, Truman Capote and James Jones made famous the old Bobby Van's in Bridgehampton. Visit the Green River Cemetery in Springs and along with Pollock and his wife Lee Krasner, you will find A. J. Liebling, Jean Stafford and Frank O'Hara. Indeed, the literary list runs long and celebrated on the East End as anyone knows who goes to the Meet the Writers Benefit at the Elaine Benson Gallery every May.

While the art and literary crowd contains a fluctuating and luminous claim to the area, the locals—or Bonackers as the old fishing and farming families call themselves—comprise, as they have for 300 years, the backbone of the community. Bonackers (from the Indian place name Accabonac) trace their ancestors to the first settlers who came here in 1640 from Maidstone, England. Anyone after that is a newcomer, plain and simple. Yet, regardless of how long we've lived here and what we do with our lives, we are all united in a passion about the place.

In our community, reflecting this passion, there is a quirky, small, independent television station known as LTV—an electronic soapbox for East End concerns, a treasure trove of creative expression, a visual and oral archive of a place, its history, its people, its beauty. LTV (the "L" stands for local) is one of the few public access stations in the country that is operated solely by the people of the community. We are homegrown television with a twist because home just happens to be one of the last great places on earth.

LTV houses over 10,000 video tapes in its library. There, baymen chronicle an oral history of the sea, historians tell us of the Shinnecocks and Montauket Indian tribes, of pirate treasure on Gardiner's Island, and Sag Harbor's raucous whaling days.

At LTV, artists explore their craft, writers read from their works, naturalists teach, and local government records the minutes of its business. On LTV there are Santa parades and school plays, high school sports and call-in shows, gospel choirs and political debates, homework hotlines and community news—and much talk about everything we are and everything we want to be.

It took two years to build and furbish the house and its fourteen rooms. What interests the creators of the doll house is not so much the exactness of scale, or strict adherence to a style but the fantasy of creating a placeless and timeless world. As you "tour" the house in these pages you will see that many of the details of the fittings and decorations are unique—the inlaid floors were hand set square by square, the curtains, cushions and bed covers were sewn from antique fabrics, the carpet in the Drawing Room was designed and needlepointed for the room as were the tiles in the fireplace each one painted and fired expressly for this house.

Perhaps the most unique aspect of the house's contents are the original paintings and sculptures by East End artists. Their works are small, invigorating delights lending a certain eclectic and rakish charm to each room. All the canvases were individually framed by our curator.

The publication of a book on the doll house presented a whole new dimension to the project. The photographs and design had to capture visually the wit and charm and detail of the house. The text wanted to capture its personality. We invited a number of our resident writers to view the house and then asked them to write whatever it inspired. The results are a mercurial collection of stories, poems and essays interwoven throughout the book—some of them pertain to this particular house, others spin off into childhood memories, notions of small and uninhibited imaginings.

The making of the Doll House and preparing this book has truly been a labor of love and a great deal of fun for many talented people. To all, I extend my personal thanks as well as the thanks of a grateful LTV. But most especially we applaud Joanna Rose whose on-going support of East End artists and writers along with her continuing support of LTV deserves our utmost regard and appreciation. Thanks to her all proceeds from the sale of this book will benefit LTV.

I hope you will enjoy your visual and literary tour of The Doll House.

Genie Chipps Henderson
President, LTV

1 THE GROUND FLOOR
Welcome to our house

Mommy, who's this doll house for?
I can't squeeze dolly through the door!

William Rossa Cole

THE ENTRANCE HALL

The solemnity of a stately grandfather's clock is offset by the gaiety of peacock feathers in a Chinese vase.
At Christmas, a creche from the Argentine is displayed for all to see.

THE DRAWING ROOM

A richly furnished formal room, it reflects the exquisite taste and varied artistic pursuits of the family. The pictures, portraits of ancestors and treasures from abroad have been in the family for ages, but the artistic place of honor goes to a romantic and intense sunset over the fireplace by Ian Hornak.

The ceramic fireplace tiles are hand-painted after a William Morris design, fired and glazed by Greg Therriault. The coffee table is painted by an artisan from Sudeley Castle Designs in the English Cotswolds. The intricate carpet was needlepointed by Alexandra Leigh-Hunt based on the colors and designs of similar carpets seen in William Morris's London house.

Three Romances for Violin and Piano by Robert Schumann inspired this musical setting. Note the hand-set inlaid flooring which compliments the dark wood paneling of the room.

DRAWING ROOM
Details

The brocade *tendu* on the walls came from the Piazza di Spagna in Rome. The painting on the right is *Gold Nocturne* by Cynthia Knott.

The bell jar was made in the Victorian era and passed down in the family collection. The geodes were found on an expedition to the mineral rich state of Utah.

Happy Christmas! The lights from the tree cast a glow on an abundance of toys and gifts which include a child's fire engine c. 1920.

Fabric for the curtains (indeed all the lace, silks and ribbons found in the stitchery of the house) are part of an antique collection inherited by Alexandra Leigh-Hunt from her mother, the famous Parisian hostess Louise de Vilmorin.

To the right of the window is Ken Robbins' hand-colored photograph *Kayenta Megalith*. Below it is *Quelques Fleurs d'Original* by Michelle Murphy. To the left: *Portrait of a Young Girl* after William Holman Hunt and *Nocturne in Blue and Silver; the Thames Estuary* after James McNeill Whistler, both by Priscilla Bowden.

THE BILLIARDS ROOM

A freshly stocked drinks table awaits the billiards players in a era long before the threat of endangered species. Inset (above) are *Tiny Maiden* by Kathe Tanous and *Blue Nocturne* by Cynthia Knott. The third painting is a reproduction of *The Rake's Progress* by Hogarth.

THE DINING ROOM

In 1922, Howard Carter opened King Tutankhamen's tomb and the world went mad for all things Egyptian. Bold spinsters journeyed down the Nile, kept copious diaries and sent crates of trinkets and artifacts home to the less adventurous. Here in the dining room, the wall borders are from an Egyptian design collection in the British Museum and are repeated in the fireplace screen. On the table, the set of serving utensils came from a curio shop in the ancient city of Thebes (now Luxor). The fish, however, was caught in Scotland.

THE MAIDS' TALE

Sheridan Sansegundo

Seventy years have gone by since my sister and I climbed the steps of that great pink mansion looking for work. By today's standards, I suppose we worked like dogs, but then Minnie and I had never known anything else. Back in County Monaghan, on a small, bleak, northfacing farm where only briars flourished and the sole excitement was Sunday Mass and the annual visit of the pig killer, we rose before dawn and had no rest until dark.

Turnips and chickens, pigs and potatoes were the entire compass of our lives, and, as our father could not afford to give us a bride price, there was little chance of change. So Minnie and I packed our few bits and pieces in a cardboard suitcase and left for America.

You can't imagine the impression the house made on us, two Irish girls who had never

THE DINING TABLE

The table is set with fine English china, silver goblets and Irish linens. The bowl of peaches, including the tiny wedges on the plate, are the handwork of a miniature artisan who specializes in one-of-a-kind fruits and flowers.

been in a building with a staircase, let alone a telephone, and who had never seen a painting, except for a few holy pictures of the Sacred Heart or St. Anthony of Padua.

It was a treasure house of strange and unfathomable objects. There were paintings of completely naked women, lamps of iridescent glass, beds so soft it was like floating in milk and, above all, a miraculous billiard table. When no one was looking, I would rest my cheek on the baize and breathe in its greenness and the perfection of the cool, heavy, gem-colored balls.

We still rose before dawn, but now it was to race to the kitchen range, which we had banked the night before in the hope that it would stay alight until morning. If it went out it was the devil's own job to get going, and cook would get as mad as a flea and rap our knuckles with a wooden spoon.

When we first arrived, she sat us down at the well-scrubbed kitchen table and gave us a mug of tea and a talk about men. We looked at her doubtfully. Just under six foot in her thick lisle stockings and "beef to the heels like a Mullingar heifer," she didn't exactly inspire belief in her wide sexual experience.

But it wasn't the lads who came courting that she warned against, it was the master himself, and though Minnie and I always managed to skip out of his clutches, there were others who didn't try so hard. Tripping up the stairs to the studio came one pretty artist's model after another. And then, after nights when the sound of angry fighting between the master and his wife seeped up to our little cots in the attic, they would disappear, with only a half-finished drawing as proof of their presence.

We would light the fires, carry the breakfast trays, do the washing, scour the pots, and never stop until it was time to sleep. How I loved the polishing. Carrying my cleaning box, with its sweet-scented beeswax for furniture and chalky pink brass polish, I would burnish everything in sight until I could see my beaming face. I was as happy as a turnip in a wet July.

In the evenings, we would open the door to splendid men in evening clothes and beauties in beaded dresses and soft curling ostrich feathers. Standing unnoticed in a sea of chatter and laughter, we waited to take their hats and perfumed furs. But by midnight the gods and goddesses were often drunk, staggering and falling on the front steps or, worse, pawing and panting on the heap of coats on the beds.

Then came the market crash of 1929 and within a few weeks all the servants were dismissed. For some years I would pass by the house, with its long elm-shaded driveway, on my way to work in a dry goods store. Each year there was more evident decay, the pink stucco faded to gray, and eventually the hedges ran so wild that the house disappeared from view.

Now I find myself trying to recall the family. It was, after all, five years of my life at an impressionable age that I spent with them, and I can remember every detail of the house itself vividly—the rock crystals in the living room, the white wicker chairs in the sun room, the photographs in the study. But yet I cannot remember their faces. Who were they? What were their names?

I asked Minnie the other day and she could not remember either, though she remembers the house in as great a detail as I do. She insists, however, that it was the wife who was the painter. The husband was a doctor, she says, a stuffy, religious type who would never have thrown wild parties. She vaguely remembers prayer meetings, and a handsome son who loved fishing.

We are both very old, of course, and it may be that memory is playing tricks on one of us. But at our age all we have left are the mysteries of the past—where people seldom were as they first appeared and old acquaintances often changed beyond recognition. That Minnie and I each seem to have furnished the pink house with a different cast of characters is just one more mystery to add to the list. ◆

THE KITCHEN

Here is the heart of the house bursting with culinary activity. The Aga stove (cook's pride) keeps everything hot and bubbling. The biscuit tins are English, as are the preserve jars and various utensils. The pottery pitcher above the stove is an American antique.

REFLECTIONS ON A DOLLHOUSE

Silvia Tennenbaum

The first doll houses—or Baby Houses, as they were then called—were fashioned in northern Europe as reproductions of actual homes. Those that survive preserve the domestic landscape in which our ancestors played out their lives so many centuries ago. They show us the shapes and configurations of ordinary things, more steadfast and substantial even than in a painting by Vermeer or Chardin. They give us a sense of that tranquil domain, presided over by women and domestics, which supports the "history" that lies, we're told, in the clamor of battles and the deposition of kings.

Gazing at the austerely classical facade of the doll house, I suddenly recall my grandparents' villa in Frankfurt am Main. It is the only one of the many houses haunting my memory that's veiled in mystery; it holds a secret I'll not uncover, unless I can trace my way back through its rooms. It was my first place of refuge—the Germans say *Geborgenheit*—and love.

(Every now and then a word in my mother tongue trips into my head and spirits me away to a lost paradise.)

Those rooms were full of light, until my grandmother's illness and death, my grandfather's suicide, darkened them. A short time later their shutters closed forever. The barbarians, marching to the sound of martial music, beneath a sea of black swastikas on white and blood-red flags, breached the walls of the formal garden. We surrendered the house to them. Its sale to the Nazis yielded precious little recompense, but we went safely to the New World.

(The end of 300 years of our history was at hand.)

The villa is gone—bombed to bits and pieces in the last year of the war, as American planes rained nightly destruction on the city. When the fighting was over, title to the rubble-strewn lot reverted to my mother and her siblings. They sold the property to speculators for a handful of silver. Two gleaming pink glass skyscrapers—headquarters of the Deutsche Bank—now stand on that very spot.

I have returned to the site more than once—an archeologist hoping to find some trace of the past. There is none. All I have to whet my memory is a watercolor of the house drawn by my grandmother, and a photo of me, on its steps, at the age of three, in a black velvet Italian urchin's costume my mother had worn to children's revels, long ago. Try as I might to reconstruct it, the villa's interior remains shrouded in shadow. I see only my grandmother's sunlit room, in which—bedridden—she spent her last months while I drew pictures, sitting quietly on the bed beside her. (So I was told.)

By then we had moved to an apartment where I sailed like a pirate on a scatter rug across the sea of blue linoleum in my room. In due time I embarked on a voyage across the real ocean, not on a magic carpet but on a large ocean liner. The world we left behind folded in upon itself and died, but my mother's hand covered my eyes and ears so I would know nothing of it.

We settled into a neo-colonial house in surburban New Rochelle, where my new life began. I wanted so desperately to be "at home" at last, that I ran like the wind from the discomposed past, from any hint of my history. But the past surrounded us, in everything we'd brought along: our clothes, our language, our *Weltanschauung*, the furniture that had graced my grandparents' villa. The Lone Ranger's cry of "Heigh-ho Silver!" rang through rooms filled with German antiques and a handful of modern Bauhaus relics.

"My mother walks with me through the rooms of an empty house. A house I've never seen in a town I do not know. I am relieved. I thought she was dead, but she isn't. She stands beside me in a room as clear and desolate as the spaces in a house painted by Edward Hopper."

I wrote these lines some years after my mother died, in an essay that evolved from journal entries made while she lay in a coma, during the last week of her life. Her death had stripped bare the rooms of all my houses.

(Are the Hopperian spaces America? Solitary, empty of the past, devoid of community. Ghost towns, the dusty crossroads of *The Last Picture Show*. East Hampton after the deluge.)

It took me some time to furnish the house once more. Looking for traces of my past, I started to write seriously for the first time. I needed to create my own world and that world, I have come to realize, is a work of the imagination. It is like the doll house whose facade reminds me of my grandparents' villa: a stage across whose boards I move my characters. For some it may become a prison, for others a comfort, for me, the writer, a work of art. Or so I hope.

Dollhouses reflect illusion and reality. The product of our machinations, they comprise a universe of which we are master. Here God reaches out to give life to Adam or to bring the wrath of His Last Judgment upon mankind. A giant thumb gently nudges a table, a hand lifts the liveried servant from his place by the sideboard.

My mother now rarely comes to me in my dreams, but I dream of houses still. Most often the house is my own, but why has it been vandalized, taken from me by rude strangers? What has happened to cause destruction in the rooms of my dreams? Is it old age approaching, my own death? The fear of losing the power of my imagination, the light of reason and certitude?

I study the doll house, thinking back, sifting through history seeking the "Ur-house" for which I yearn. Soon I shall travel one more time. Searching for home in the great spaces of this continent and the old world. Once upon a time I learned that freedom lies in sailing across the blue ocean or driving a car through the landscape that stretches to the western skies. I've always found a place to rest my head at the end of the day, a room to make my own to start anew. If you aren't home, any *house* will do. As long as it has a view.

But will I ever find those rooms of love again? ◆

CHILD'S PLAY

Marjorie Appleman

Her summer world gone topsy-turvy:
dining rooms inside-out,
bathrooms outside-in,
kitchens upside-down,
drawing rooms downside-up.
In her doll house
she dances from space
to space, standing still.

The princess is all alone, waiting,
trapped in the body of a girl.

She frets about the mother queen,
shut inside the master bedroom,
spell-struck, needing rescue from
the hands of tooth wizards.
The father king,
charmed by the head sorcerer,
sits chained to his desk in the study
where books bind.
The brother prince,
possessed by one wicked witch
after another, daily
betrays her.

How can the trance be ended?

Moon wakes her to a sky
full of cat howls and dark wings,
Sun burns her to sleep again, friends
play tricks on her and cannot be found.
She lives with strangers
who take her for someone else,
her dog will not come when she calls,
but runs out the entrance hall,
she chases after, and finds

tree-blossoms, weed-flowers,
blue clouds in a new lake.

She swims with minnows and tadpoles,
wishing for a change,
she sings with birds and bugs,
wanting to be heard,
she throws magic stones in
magic water, makes
magic rings.

Who will break the spell?

On a gray day a breeze comes out to play
tag with the rain
and catches her by surprise:
        She's it.
    A robin sings the signal:
        Ready.
    A frog in disguise jumps:
        Get set.
    A dragon flies past her face:
        Wait.
    She scans the bushy moat around the castle,
    a wand of light beams down,
    her spy in the enemy camp barks:
        Go!
    She runs straight for the gate.

Inside, in the dark, is
the one she has to save,
the one who holds the key:
the silent queen.

Is it child's play, hide and seek?
A game of life
and death?

PORTRAIT

Barbara Thompson

When I met Bradley Muir he was already an old man, gaunt and harrowed, heavy with late honors. His great work was behind him—the Civil War tetralogy, an encoded narration of his wife's Virginia forebears, and the pair of linked novels about World War II set in a Sussex village where bombs never fell, from which the garrisoned Yanks departed for Normandy only on the last page. Like his idol James, he was a master at conveying violent events through the vibrations of trees and masonry a hundred miles away.

In the beginning he was my teacher. I was an overage divorced graduate student before that became ordinary, clumsily balancing school and a job and an irritable twelve-year-old daughter; he and Winifred took me in as they might have taken in an attractive animal witlessly declawed. I chose to write my thesis on his English novels, as much out of filial as literary devotion.

When I told him, Bradley asked me what I knew about snipe shooting. Nothing, of course. "The snipe is a bird without talon or extraordinary speed, but he has evolved his own means of persisting to live: he varies his flight with a random display of balletics: little circles, dives, jinks to one side. To bring him down you need to intuit his pattern, not his direction but the bit of dance he will do next." It was a warning I only half understood—Bradley's loquaciousness was as likely to obscure as explain. All he meant to tell was on the page.

"Were you stationed in Sussex during the War?"

"Surrey. But it doesn't matter. The house was Irish. When they did the limited edition the artist must have copied something from a rotogravure. It isn't my house."

"And the family, was there a particular model?"

"The Brits were kind to us, at least in my experience. We were a tiny group, and rather indrawn for soldiers—one fellow was a botanist, he did nothing but catalogue ragweed. We didn't make ourselves offensive, and so they were good to us, Sunday dinners and that sort of thing.

"In one house I was given the freedom of the library, an extraordinary collection over three or four generations: editions of Trollope as they came out, Hollinshead, Shakespeare with steel engravings from the great 19th century performances."

"Were there young people around, someone your own age?"

"The elder son was in the RAF. I never met him, I think he was captured in the first months' fighting. And there was a sister still at home, and a charming younger son, Harry, who came back only during school holidays. I wonder what happened to him . . . He had that precision of speech that only English schoolboys possessed."

"You dedicated the second volume of your War novel to someone named Lavinia—"

"My grandmother's name was Lavinia. There's a little oval miniature of her somewhere. Ask Winifred." And he would be off—to the University, or the Library, or somewhere else where he could not be followed.

So I looked at his grandmother's generic oval face in the gilded oval frame, at photograph albums, shoeboxes of vacation snapshots—some from Surrey after the War—until I realized that they yielded up nothing without some decoding device, which I lacked. Even the room in which I scrutinized all these artifacts was dominated by an undecipherable artifact, the nearly life-sized portrait of a grave young girl with chestnut hair held back by combs or a dark ribbon. Her dress revealed no date; only her gaze, the set of her soft jaw seemed modern. The portrait hung high on the wall in the fashion of an earlier time; it should have been inconspicuous there, with its browns and dusty chiaroscuro, far above the lamplight, but in fact it commanded the room. Who was she?

"I don't know," Winifred Muir said. "Bradley bought it with a lot of other things, at auction." Her jaw seemed to click shut, denying further interrogation.

I went on with my work without much help from Bradley Muir, but once he saw that I had given up ferreting out his sources, we fell back into the old ways. I became a kind of adopted daughter, though I stepped carefully, an orphan taken in late enough to know the reversibility of grafts.

Winifred died first, so silently in the night that Bradley, sleeping next to her, woke at his regular hour only to find her long past wakening. If that stealthy death frightened him—he was the "sick" one with a bad heart, ten years her senior—he never said so. "That is the bed she brought into the marriage," he said. "We slept in it for more than forty years. She had hoped our children would be born in that bed."

I helped him sort her things. It was surprising how little there was, in that cluttered house, that was personal to her. All but the bed, which would go after Bradley's death, we sent to a nephew of hers in Richmond: some anniversary jewelry, amethyst and sapphire, her wedding pearls and her high-pronged engagement diamond, some inherited mourning pieces from the last century made of onyx and human hair. There were hand-pieced quilts, dated and signed in chain stitch with her maiden name, evening dresses in heavy velvet I could not bear to send to the Salvation Army, and pieces of lace, one like a field of butterflies, folded in black tissue, that was her wedding veil.

Bradley was almost ninety now, but he held on, not writing but dictating sometimes into a little machine that an admirer had given him and a graduate student hooked up next to his bed. He did not sleep much, and there were still many stories to tell, if not to write. On the tape you can hear him shaping them as he goes, long pauses as the paragraphs gather in his mind before he tells them to the little black ear.

I came every afternoon at three to help him with his mail—invitations, unsolicited manuscripts from strangers, galleys from publishers seeking a quotable line for some acquaintance's dust jacket, letters telling of the deaths of friends. I opened everything now. "All my secrets are in the past" he said once, looking at me in a slant way. "You won't let some biographer roust them out when I'm gone, will you?"

And then one day, not in their musty, lavender-scented marriage bed but in an ambulance screaming toward the University hospital, he was gone.

The Richmond nephew came for the service with a wife and two little girls in pastel shades of organdy, and after the prayers and the sherry, he took the bed and a few other pieces of furniture in a rented van. The rest would be appraised and the valuable things sent to auction. His books and papers had already been given to the University, and a few days after the service a young man arrived to help me sort and pack. I was to be literary executor and for my pains given the pick of what remained.

There were few surprises. Bradley Muir was a man of orderly ways: no one pawing through his papers would find an unaccountable woman's name or reference to a drunken indiscretion. But his desk had a secret compartment, it turned out, typical of its era: when you withdrew the shallow drawer, there was a boxed space beyond, deeper and as wide. It contained two things, a snapshot of a slim dark-haired girl in a WAF uniform, and a line-a-day diary from the years 1940–1945.

His handwriting in the diary was crisp and firm, but the ink, grown pale, was hard to read. Notations for 1940 and 1941 were brief, as the design imposed. On his wedding day, June 12, 1941, he wrote only "4 o'clock, St Peter's. *Joy!*"

But by the end of 1942, the entries grew less frequent and often covered several pages. They listed books read and charted friendships he had struck up, first with the village vicar and later, through the vicar's intervention, with a family named St. John. Late in October of 1943 he began to make architectural drawings, detailed and to scale, and drawings of pieces of furniture. Even paintings were indicated, landscapes and portraits and glassy-eyed domestic animals.

After a while I saw the purpose of this work, which at first I had taken to be a series of sketches for some never-written work of fiction (for these were not the rooms of his English novel): I was at that very moment sitting in the little sketched study, at a desk identical but for minor detail to the one on the page. The moldings he had drawn in 1943 were above me now, as in the parlor the paintings were "skyed" in the Victorian way, the furniture placed as it had been in the house he sketched more than fifty years ago in Surrey.

I walked through the rooms again, softly as though there were people in them who must not be disturbed. The graduate student called out to me, then by whatever intuition fell silent in midsentence. I felt as though I had come out into the daylight after an intense afternoon in the theater or a movie show: my realities were disjunctive. Was this house then a shrine of some sort, or was it just an inexperienced young man's emulation of an adult world he had admired and wanted for himself? What had Winifred known, or shared, or felt?

I made a pot of strong black tea for the two of us, and got the graduate student to sit with me for a while and talk about commonplace things. He was as shy as he had been the first day, but agreeable, malleable; he asked nothing. But before he went back to boxing up the books, I had him bring the ladder in from the garage and take down the heavier paintings for me.

I was only a little surprised to find Bradley Muir's youthful block printing on the wooden stretcher of the portrait of the young woman with chestnut hair who so possessed the drawing room. "Lavinia St. John, 1938", it said. "Bought through Fowlers, London, July, 1947". Stilling envy, I took it for my legacy.♦

2 UPSTAIRS
The private family rooms

THE STUDY

T o write is to write is to write is to write is to write is to write is to write.

—Gertrude Stein

A room of one's own (or even a hallway) becomes the writer's hideaway. Here the disheveled desk, jammed file cabinet, and overflowing waste basket tell of the struggle to place words on paper.

THE
STUDY

Literary Inspiration comes from the surround of books and photographs. Among them, Daisy Ashford, author of *The Young Visiters* (sic), Oscar Wilde, William Morris and a woodcut from the pages of William Blake. The elusive muse may even be found in *Wooden Angel*, the black and white silver print by Gerry Giliberti.

THE GENTLEMAN'S DRESSING ROOM

Reflecting manly interests in sport and game, this room houses a collection of sporting prints and paintings along with a bagged moose from the deep woods of Nova Scotia.

In the bathing closet is a handpainted zinc tub c. 1890. The English setter is holding a newspaper which headlines the sinking of the Titanic.

The hip waders are hand crafted by an artisan in Virginia and the model ship comes from a ship's chandler in Stonington, Maine.

Above photograph includes *Fabian's Folly With Groom* after George Stubbs and *Landscape: Perugia* after Edward Lear, both by Priscilla Bowden.

THE
BLUE
BEDROOM

The mural, which covers all four walls, is "A Panorama of Bembridge: Isle of Wight in 1800" painted by Edward Francis Burney (1760–1848) and reproduced from the original watercolor found in the Victoria & Albert Museum.

The bed is a piece de resistance of antique laces, silks and ribbons sewn by Alexandra Leigh-Hunt, as are the hat, cushions and curtains. The Staffordshire dogs on the faux marble mantle and the pitcher and basin on the wash stand are English. The brocade carpet is one of a pair in the house and was bought from a vendor at the Spanish Steps in Rome.

From
"LITTLE FOLLIES"

Eric Kraft

At about the time that I began work on "The Static of the Spheres," Albertine brought home two large cartons of wood from which she planned to build a miniature of Small's Hotel. She had in mind a true miniature, not just a represen tation of the exterior. She would build with miniature framing, tiny nails, sheathing, and clapboards. Best of all, she bought a set of tiny, precise tools: a square, a plane, saws with teensy teeth, a mitre box, and so on.

She was at work on her small hotel throughout my work on this, and I suppose that the rhythms of her min-

THE BATHROOM

In England, the bath can take up much of the morning as one luxuriates in deep tubs scented with French toilet waters. Here one can contemplate Francesco Bologna's "Dory" (far right) or Edward Lear's series of bird prints. The William Morris screen is also imprinted with birds.

iature construction—the tap-tap-tap of her little hammer, the back-and-forth whisper of her little saw—underlie some passages. But that is by the way; I want to say something about the materials themselves.

When she brought the stuff home, we spread it out neatly on the tabletops in the dining room and spent quite a while just handling all of it and looking at it.

"You know, Al," I said to her. "this is just like the moment when Guppa has all the parts of the radio lined up on his workbench. I have the same anticipatory feelings, the same mixture of excitement, eagerness—and fear. I sense, in all this cute stuff you brought home, what I should sense in the parts of the radio when they lie in ranks on Guppa's workbench—the presence of a potential magnificence, something that I've found in the parts of other things before they're assembled. The components might be—oh—a clutter of memories, boxes full of thin slabs of basswood and slender dowels, or ranks of vacuum tubes, resistors, capacitors, transformers, and the like. Sleeping in these things is the capacity to become a book, a dollhouse, or a shortwave receiver. One has the feeling that merely by gathering the parts, one has made a step toward realizing the end.

" 'Ah,' one is tempted to say, 'the pieces are all there. Now all I have to do is put them together.' "

"But—" I said, dramatically, "—it may be better, sometimes, to leave the pieces as they are, unassembled, for the potential book crackles with wit, the shutters on the potential dollhouse are straight, and the signals picked up by the potential receiver are clear and strong, but the actual book is going to have its passages of half-baked philosophy and weepy sentimentality, some of the shutters on the actual dollhouse will hang at odd angles, and the receiver may bring in nothing but a rising and falling howl muffled by a thick hiss."

Al laughed at me and told me to get upstairs and get to work, and I did. ◆

THE GIRL'S ROOM

A room for a darling daughter who, all too soon, will be sent to Switzerland to be finished. When she returns, the charming toys of childhood will have been packed away for future children.

The bronze wheeled ox is from India. The ceramic mouse and camel were carried home from a long-ago trip to China. The doll in the cradle was whittled in the hills of Kentucky.

The wallpaper border is by Kate Greenaway. Prints are from Beatrix Potter. On the left is Degas' *Dancer* by printmaker Ryna Segal.

MOTHER SAID:

Siv Cedering

T ake care of the dolls.
At night they talk
about naked limbs,
unblanketed beds,
heads twisted
backwards.

Father said:
when you make a fire
in the woods,
don't quench it
completely, leave it
for the little people.

I leave the fire in the woods.

I listen to the dark.

47

THE CONSER-VATORY

A private room where the family can retreat for tea and enjoy their eclectic collection of art. Prominent is the wood sculpture in the style of the great Brancusi by William King. To the right of the door hangs *Big Sur,* a collage by Nan Orshefsky. To the left of the curio cabinet is *Mondrian* by Dana Westring. On the outside wall hangs *Suzie D's Manner* by Connie Fox.

The curio cabinet (detailed later in the book) contains shells from Sanibel Island, coral, rocks from Nova Scotia and a fossil ammonite from the beach at Lyme Regis, England.

The Chinese teapot is antique.

PALE, BRIGHT DAY

Joe Pintauro

June 24th, 1934, 11:45 p.m.
Dear Diary,
I thought that adulthood would be a boring curse, but tonight being twenty-one is the most divine blessing of my life. A large moon is pressing on my screens, yet I'm writing in shadow. A light seems to be guiding me from within.

I've seen a whole year of light in one day, starting with the moment Joanna Halsey stepped into our living room, dressed in white (not for mother's "white garden" tea; she'd been to a wedding). Joanna was such a resplendent vision that my sister Fannie's face fell apart when she came into the room.

"How conceited of Joanna to upstage mother's flowers," Fannie spewed forth. I forgive my sister. I do. Fannie's been nervous over simply having had one silly date with Nick Winslow. She begged mother not to mention the flowers in the invitations for fear it would rain, for fear there would be too few white blooms, for fear that we would seem pretentious, for fear Nick Winslow would think us gauche, though there were more white roses on the vines today than ever.

White was in the brilliant clouds, and silvery white wherever the sun touched, but the brightest vision of all was Joanna. (She had caught the bridal bouquet at Blackie Latham and Sarah Griswold's wedding in Southampton.) Joanna was prettier than a bride in her white shoes and stockings, prettier than Sarah Latham could hope to be in a thousand years and with infinitely more pluck.

The moon has entered the room somehow and now the rug's ablaze. I'll explode with joy if the day doesn't end soon. Only the weeping sounds coming from Fannie's room keep me from floating up through the roof. Poor thing. Nick Winslow never showed up.

But I was happy for mother. Her irises were crisp and snowy with green throats and white beards, just as in the catalogue. I had spent all yesterday picking off rotting blossoms and repainting the arbors and mother's wooden jardinieres. If only Fannie could have tucked her jealousy away somewhere. She made a rude pout when Joanna merely asked to borrow a comb. The Halseys had just driven down from the wedding in an open car.

"The bride should have been furious with her wearing white. She looks like a nurse," Fannie said aloud. "And she's making eyes at you! Don't fall for her manipulations." Of course I fell for them, but not without shame. See January 11 notation (I had skated up to Joanna on the ice pond and invited her to go 'round and she flew off, saying she was with Blackie Latham). But this afternoon she offered her most alluring smile and . . . how could I not smile back, for God's sake, Fannie? I was delighted to fall for her "manipulations." Delighted and, for the moment, drunkenly in love with Joanna Halsey all over again. Oh God! Did I say that?

She had found comfort in the dark of our living room, where she had turned to me with what seemed almost tearful eyes and said, "I love this house." As if it were a place from her own past. I offered to show her the upstairs and she followed me, adoring each room, removing her gloves and touching everything with tenderness. Coming down, she stopped mother.

"How quaint your house is," she said. "Quaint? Quaint?" mother responded, obviously put off. "But of course you're used to much more."

"Oh, but 'grand' would do your home a disservice." Joanna's eyes became wide as dinner plates. "This is the most stunningly cozy and beautiful house I have ever ever had the honor to be invited to—really. Our house is too drafty and ongoing, so vacant and forbidding that I feel lost except in my room. And your white garden is too lovely for words, almost lovelier than the house to which it is perfectly matched."

"Thank you," mother gasped as if she'd just won the sweepstakes. "Now you," she turned to me, "don't let Joanna tramp around our grass in those pretty shoes. Drive her into town and treat her to an ice cream soda or something. On with you."

Joanna whispered something to Mrs. Halsey, picked up Sarah Griswold's wedding bouquet and drove us to Gordon's Bar in Amagansett where the bartender knew her. Joanna downed a Side Car then drove me to the ocean, where she removed her shoes and stockings and ran ahead into the foamy surf, not minding that she was wetting her dress at the hem.

Then, rejoining me, she mentioned rather casually that she and Blackie Latham were always "as brother and sister." I asked her if she was seeing anyone at the moment. "Yes, at the moment. . . ." She smiled.

"Who?" I asked, with a lump in my throat.

"At the moment I'm seeing you. Or am I being presumptuous?"

"Well, no. No, not presumptuous." I stammered. "But you are also seeing the surf and the sky and that silly man running into those icy waves in the moment and a moment is too brief. That's all I'm saying." She had me totally in her power. Then, swinging wildly away from me, she flung Sarah's wedding bouquet into the surf, then put her fingers to her lips in a tearful prayer. The undertow tumbled the bouquet back to her feet, shining and full of foam. I bent to pick it up.

"No," she said. "Leave it."

I placed a hand comfortingly on her shoulder, not knowing what she might be feeling. She slipped from under it and ran, facing Montauk. Then she turned and cried out, "Do you like me?"

"You know I do," I called back.

It was all I could do not to scream a shout of implausible happiness and gratitude that Joanna Halsey existed in this world and that I was with her in that gorgeous day. I took her hand strongly, as if I hadn't given it a moment's thought, although I had, and her response was not to disallow it, but to squeeze my hand as if she intended to keep it forever. We said nothing as we walked. We had already indicated too much. But I hereby declare this the happiest day of my life. And it was so far so unexpected and simple.

There's something new about me. I'm really not so bad-looking as I thought. In the mirror, I see a more handsome fellow than I was and I would not change my face for any man's, ever. Still, I'm sad for Fannie's unfathomable misery, for this new summer that will be old too soon, for mother's garden, which will waste in the fall, but especially I'm sad for this sweet house in which I was born, knowing someday soon, because of Joanna Halsey, I shall have to leave it forever.

But my happiness eclipses every sad thought tonight and I swear, to God in heaven, I shall never let this day's light grow old inside me.

Stay tuned. D. ◆

A ROOM IS A WOMB IS A ROOM

Kennett Love

Tiny people—fairies, imps, Teeny-Weenies, hobbits, gremlins, the Lilliputians, all the homunculi—have fascinated humans of all ages throughout the ages. We love to imagine their habitations, burrows, a shoe, engine crevices, whole cities of Lilliputians.

Doll houses, especially, and ship models are places where we imagine them living and working, winding their tiny grandfather clocks, pedalling their tiny sewing machines, hauling on their hair-thin halyards. Looking into the LTV doll house is a supernatural experience, like seeing through roofs and walls from the night sky.

Which of all those tiny rooms could I be happy in? Rooms, rooms, great and small. Up there in the night sky of the mind, other rooms scrolled before me. A room means an enclosed shelter. Room rhymes with womb, the shelter where every one of us entered life, where we lived as tiny people for nine months on the first leg of the journey.

The roots of the two words are different, but there is a conceptual similarity between them and a mystical link that goes back through the millennia.

The connection became part of a traditional Christian image, wrote the scholar John Gross, "repeated by countless writers, contrasting the infinitude of Christ's power with the 'little room' of the Virgin's womb."

That room, little though it be, is replete with all that is needed for the first part of the journey—food, warmth, protection—all so perfectly metered and immediate that the very idea of need would be incomprehensible to a thinking occupant.

We never find its like again. But we try. I came nearest to it in the cabin of the Windrover, a Concordia yawl in which I sailed the seas for nearly a decade, including a winter voyage from Monterey, California, to Hawaii and back. The cabin was down a companionway from the vast room of the welkin, six or seven miles from horizon to horizon with the sky for a ceiling, a wood-walled room of my own in the mansion of the universe.

It was the room in which I came to Sag Harbor on June 12, 1979, after beating from Montauk Point into a cold, blue-sky northwesterly gale. More than any of my many other lodgings, it gave me an embryo's certainty of its place in the universe and contentment at being there. My sextant came out of its cupboard at first light, when the horizon becomes visible and the height of the stars above it can be measured. Three of them were enough to tell me where I was.

Without this peripatetic room of my own, would I ever have fetched up on the East End of Long Island and seen the wonderful world of the LTV doll house? You can stare into it for hours and have such thoughts! ♦

A FEW WORDS ABOUT DOLL HOUSES
Arthur Prager

Doll houses have always been the quintessential toy, enjoyed by children and grown-ups of every age and quality, passed from generation to generation with improvements or battle scars until they fall apart. They are never out of fashion. The Greeks and Romans had them and so did the Egyptians. The children of prehistoric cave people undoubtedly had completely furnished doll caves.

Let's face it, there is a certain amount of gender discrimination connected with them, but of a benevolent, harmless kind. If little girls enjoy playing with them while little boys prefer fire engines, what's the harm in that?

Miniaturization has often had a religious, sometimes even occult connotation. Tiny creatures and their household chattels were said in fairy tales and legends to have magical powers. In bedtime stories, toys often come to life after dark and have mysterious adventures of their own in which real-life children frequently take part. Miniature people and animals, dwellings, vehicles, and even money were used by the Chinese as funeral decorations, placed in the tombs of the rich to help them enjoy in paradise the things they loved in life.

Some doll houses are works of art in their own right, like the 18th-century beauty at Uppark in Warwickshire, one of the stately homes owned by the British National Trust. Everything in it is authentic and genuine. The tiny silverware is hallmarked, the crystal is Waterford, the paintings by contemporary artists, all perfect. Curiously, there are no dolls living in it, which gives it the strange lifeless emptiness of a museum exhibit, which is exactly what it is. If aristocratic children ever played with it, there are no signs of wear and tear. A more modern example is the 20th-century Stettheimer doll house, art nouveau and very 1920s, at the Museum of the City of New York.

Doll houses are sometimes elements of terror and despair, such as those used in voodoo ceremonies, or the stage miniature in Edward Albee's "Tiny Alice," visible to the audience only in its exterior elevation, but inhabited by the eponymous Alice, who moves from room to room, turning lights on and off, unavailable to her new husband, who can never enter, and to Sir John Gielgud, in the front yard intoning what must certainly be the longest death speech in theater history.

In my own experience, raising a little girl through a childhood in which dolls and their houses played an important part, I found them fascinating. One could create imaginary dramas of all kinds in those shadowy little rooms. The only disappointment was the dolls themselves, with their glassy staring eyes and immobile limbs. The houses needed sounds, cooking odors, movement, laughter and tears. My daughter didn't agree. She liked her doll house as it was, peopled not by regular dolls but by small plastic naked babies from Woolworths. They were enough for her to wrap fantasies around.

The greatest example of doll house as metaphor for despair is of course the Ibsen play, in which a toy house (although it doesn't actually appear on stage) represents the disappointment of a woman trapped in a dead-end marriage, denied what she feels are the glittering prizes of a career. Home and motherhood and a husband who regards her as a decorative plaything have (she thinks) destroyed her life. Reading "A Doll's House" as a teenager, I always thought she should have let well enough alone and enjoyed what she had instead of wanting more more more. I wished that someone (not Ibsen—Alan Ayckbourn, perhaps) had written a sequel.

Now that I have a granddaughter, the doll house cycle will begin again in a year or two, and I am looking forward to it. Dolls are more lifelike these days, though one must resist at all costs the politically correct kind. Somewhere in my attic there is a fine and delicate antique Japanese house, bought for my daughter in Taiwan, and taken apart like a finely wrought puzzle. It is very old and hand-tooled. Its occupant is a lovely little princess in an embroidered kimono, kneeling as the Japanese do instead of sitting. My granddaughter is too little to play with it now, but some day it will be there for her as a surprise. I hope she loves it as much as we did before her. ♦

3 TOP FLOOR
Castoffs and unfinished work

THE MYSTERIOUS TRUNK

B.H. Friedman

Some doll houses contain fantasies far larger than themselves: fantasies of palaces, forts, shrines; fantasies that travel great distances through time and space. Others, like the house pictured here, are as comparatively cozy and contemporary as a turn-of-the-century English country house.

Here is the luxury of space for everything—fourteen rooms, including an artist's studio, a writer's study, a dressing room, a drawing room, a billiards room, as well as an attic containing rejected furniture, silent games, tired tools, an empty birdcage, and a mysterious trunk in which there may be anything, even a tiny doll house.

I focus on the metal-clad trunk, partially covered with the labels of ocean liners and ports of call. My eyes pry open its lock and curved lid. I imagine a ledger inside, also locked, in which there is a catalogue of every object in the house, how much it cost, where it was bought.

Each piece of furniture is listed, each rug, each painting and print, each souvenir from Mexico, Egypt, China. By today's standards the prices, all carefully recorded in meticulous Victorian script, are ridiculously cheap: ten dollars for a bed, half as much for a watercolor by Whistler, pennies for a child's game.

Some of these items are already in the attic. Some have worn out. Some have been discarded or sold. Others will eventually reach there, moving slowly up through the house, over a period of years, until nothing recorded in the ledger remains downstairs, and another generation must face the emptiness of the rooms below.♦

THE ATTIC

Forgotten, stored, broken . . . here collecting dust are trunks and crates, toys and games and decades of accumulated household items long past use. But there is life in the attic . . . a mouse lives in the sofa, a dove nests in the rafters and surely there are numerous spiders in the cobwebs of the shelving.

THE ARTIST'S STUDIO

Echoes of *la vie Boheme* in the English countyside. Up the stairs from the writer's study the artist can retreat from the rigours of family life. A skylit loft recalls youthful lodging in Paris when what mattered was not warmth and food but the freedom to create. Often, there is a model who may pose from the platform or lie seductively on the divan.

The walls are covered with copies of art of the period.

The screen, behind which the model changes her clothes, is Japanese gilt.

THE ARTIST'S
STUDIO *Details*

The painting on the easel and those stacked on the floor are by Dana Westring. Inside the sketch book are figure studies by Priscilla Bowden.

A pot-bellied stove keeps away the chills of a damp winter.

By the early 20's, photography was well established as a form of artistic expression and no studio was complete without the latest model of the camera.

Among the canvases rolled in the box is *The Dance* after Matisse painted by Priscilla Bowden.

DWELLING
Fran Castan

The first house you left dreams.
    In the belly of the sink, in the eye of the glass,
in the arms of the old wing chair, it asks
"What has become of you?" It abides

like the snail's spent shell
swirled in the shape of seasons gone
and come again, as the planet whirls on
to sleep in its own shadow, only

to shine again, in the sun. You
must return to that dwelling in the dark,
take memory back,
and, this time, learn to live by heart.

BLACK TEA

Jeffrey Potter

Nora, the manor house cook, was less tyrant than monarch. Her throne was a well-cushioned armchair in the servants' dining room from which she could keep an eye on the crown jewels: one big coal range and two small maids, Molly and Dolly.

As did her other subjects, they addressed her as "Ma'am" and their bobbing curtseys were as natural as her use of the royal "we."

"In our house we'll have no manservants, devil take them," she decreed. "It's pride in hard work that makes a fine house a great one, so it will be County Cork women, all."

An exception to her edict was bashful Tim, the houseman, because of the gleam he gave to brass, floors and boots. But praise was sparse for fear of encouraging his dream of a footman's livery, heavy with shiny buttons. Out of his hearing, Nora liked telling her court that this button hope was to be expected. "Faith, and isn't he lacking all his own?"

The upstairs world called her "Mrs. Nora" and were too humbled to do more than ask, carefully, why her dishes looked so much better than they tasted.

"My dishes? It's fit for a king, they are!"

A deposed one, the upstairs told one another, and took refuge in humor. They dined out on tales of Nora's reign and quoted the bishop's suspicion that she must be an incognito member of the royalty herself. And then there was the parish priest and his gratitude for her rejection of the confessional. It would take a court chaplain to handle Nora's absolution, he thought.

The high point of the day for her subjects was four-o'clock tea in their dining room, with Nora presiding as high priestess. While Molly and Dolly brushed her long silver hair, one to a side, all eyes would be on the large earthenware tea-pot steeping the black leaves. Eventually, Nora would lift the lid to consider the brew, then perform the rite of pouring. The drinking was always hurried, for the point of the hour was her reading of the leaves in the empty cups.

"Your future is in their lying," she would remind them. "But no lying is in their message, that there isn't."

The leaves had nothing to say on days when housework was not well done, or not enough pride taken, and the silence would be broken only by sighs of longing and disappointment. But more often the leaves spoke of good futures, producing laughter, even joy. The head waitress might hear of a farm, pretty as a picture ("Oh, my"); the parlor maid would be healed of an illness to be ("Saints be praised!") or the chambermaid of a back strained from bed-making (much signing of the Cross), and the second waitress would hear of a young man to walk out with on afternoons off (giggles and "Go on, will ye!).

THE MAID'S ROOMS

She irons and sews in her bare attic room with little attention to decor. Yet the tedium of her job is alleviated by the voyeuristic entertainment of the studio next door.

The metal bedstead is by William King. The wash stand and toilet are from a c.1920 American miniature collection.

For Molly and Dolly there might be a coal range all their own in which to bake meals to sell in town, if they kept Nora's crown jewel well blacked (curtseys, low). For Tim, there would be buttons surely, but they'd be those of a lass's eyes. "And mind the front door knocker has a polish to blind us." (Forelock pulled.)

Word of Nora's readings spread through the county, bringing written requests from strangers. They went unanswered—"County fair readings are good enough for the likes of them." And the lady's maid brought an overture from upstairs (ignored)—"There's no pleasing them, their pride is of self."

But upstairs tried to win Nora over by seducing her subjects with labor-saving equipment. When a howling Hoover came in, out went the rattling O'Cedar sweeper, and, along with it, pride. Not only did a washer/dryer appear, but a powered mangle, leaving the laundress with nothing to wring but her hands. Then the waitress had to deal with treated cloths for the silver, so forget the Gorham polish and rubbing. Where is the pride there?

The chambermaid was supposed to welcome spray cans for the bathrooms—no more pride in being on her knees to scrub. Tim was given a clear lacquer to brush on all the brass, and plastic coating for the floors, leaving only boots to see himself in. The worst blow was the last: a gas cooker to replace the coal range. It put Molly and Dolly in tears, this loss of blacking and rubbing away with murmurs of sweet nothings, as to a lover.

Nora was not only outraged but the leaves wouldn't speak, which meant no futures for her subjects, or indeed for the house. Soon she was gone, without notice, followed by her retainers, to the hotel in town. There she was given a suite (a royal one, naturally) in which to live and give readings, Molly and Dolly in attendance. Tim, with no button-eyed lass yet in view, was issued a porter's jacket, with buttons shiny as they come. The others from the manor house found futures as Nora had prophesied; but they looked back on their times of hard work and pride with nostalgia.

It is said that an emissary from Buckingham Palace, in secret, approached Nora on behalf of the young royals, all but begging for a reading. He was dismissed with an airy wave of the hand by Nora, who confided in the hotel manager with a sigh.

"It's not that we are too grand to read their future, daft though they be. Faith, we've not the heart to look." ◆

ISABELLE'S HOUSE
Lou Ann Walker

"Christmas" was Isabelle Reynolds's first thought when she awoke that snowy morning. She felt the crisp winter air on her face as she twirled under the comforter. The children weren't allowed to come downstairs on Christmas morning until her mother shook the sleigh bells. Hundreds of times Isabelle had dreamed of this moment, just before she discovered the most glorious Christmas present—her doll house.

Eyes closed, Isabelle imagined herself moving tiny chairs and tables, sofas and beds. She would help her dolls light the fire and then of course she'd have to make curtains for the windows. Isabelle had sneaked down one evening after her mother and father thought she was asleep. She'd wanted a glass of milk but she overheard her parents talking in the parlor.

"Mr. Whisman says he thinks he can have

the doll house finished by the middle of December," her father said.

"Isabelle's just the right age," her mother was saying dreamily. "She's been taking such nice care of her dolls and her room. . . . I would have loved one when I was a girl."

What Isabelle didn't hear after she'd tiptoed back up the stairs was her father saying, "I hope Charlie Whisman can hold out."

Ever since, Isabelle had been planning and saving for her house. When Mrs. Bates, her neighbor, was about to throw out a scrap of yellow gingham, she asked for the piece. Isabelle found a worn-out straw broom in the trash. She broke off pieces of straw and tied them with an end of string to a twig. Her house would be clean and tidy. She tucked the fabric and the tiny twig broom under her mattress.

Sleigh bells were ringing. She flung off the covers. Holding her slippers in her hand, she raced her brother, Stephen, to the parlor where the Christmas tree nearly touched the ceiling. There were games and toys and even a baby doll's carriage. Tears started rolling down Isabelle's cheeks.

"What's the matter?" her mother asked. "Nothing," Isabelle said, trying to hold up the ends of a smile despite the fact that her face was flooded with tears. Perhaps she had misunderstood. Perhaps her father had meant Christmas next year. Still, she couldn't let on to her mother that she'd known about the doll house. Her parents would not have approved at all about eavesdropping. But Isabelle couldn't stop crying.

Worried, Mrs. Reynolds dropped to her knees. "Why are you crying?"

"Oh, mother. I'm awful. I didn't mean to. I came downstairs for some milk and I heard you and Daddy talking and I heard about a doll house and I'd gotten my hopes up and I know I was bad. It was very naughty."

"Isabelle," Dr. Reynolds said. "Intentional eavesdropping is different from accidentally overhearing." He looked at her closely. His smile was sad, too. "One of my patients was

going to make you a doll house in exchange for my treating him. But he was very, very sick and he couldn't finish."

"Well, he can finish it when you make him better, can't he?" Isabelle asked.

"I'm sorry, Isabelle. Mr. Whisman died a week ago. Your mother and I were planning on finding someone to build the doll house right after Christmas. Actually, I thought I might try it myself."

Isabelle blinked. "Thanks, Daddy," she said. But in her heart she hoped he wouldn't do it himself. He'd once built a chair for her room. It had taken days. He'd spent so much time at his workbench. The chair leaned to the left when she sat on it. She'd gotten a splinter the first day and the second day her finger began bleeding when she pricked herself on a nail.

The family was about to sit down to Christmas dinner when there was a knock. Her father opened the heavy door. "Isabelle!" her father called. Stanley Whisman, Charlie Whisman's son, was peeking over a huge parcel wrapped in an old blanket.

"My family was so grateful to your father," Stanley said. "My Dad said he just couldn't go to heaven if we didn't repay Dr. Reynolds right away. It took me a while, in between my work and all, but here it is. I think my Dad would be proud of it, God rest his soul."

Isabelle shook Stanley Whisman's hand. She'd never seen her parents look so happy. Stanley Whisman and her father carried the white doll house with green shutters right into the parlor, then Isabelle rushed upstairs to get her fabric and broom. Her mother went off to the kitchen cupboard where she'd hidden a set of tiny silver pots and pans and a little burgundy brocade sofa she'd bought. Isabelle's fingers were her dolls and Stephen didn't bother her treasures. Not even once.

* * *

In 1913, Isabelle Reynolds Clarke had a baby daughter, Hannah. Holding her tiny baby, Isabelle told her mother, "I just can't wait until she's old enough for the doll house. I'll make new cushions for the chairs and I saw the sweetest wooden canopy bed at the toy store. It will be just perfect!" But when Hannah was four, her mother died in the flu epidemic. Mrs. Reynolds took care of her granddaughter, who had Isabelle's red curls and freckles and bright blue eyes.

Mrs. Reynolds loved Hannah dearly. But she could never bring out the doll house. Just the thought of it flooded her mind with wonderful memories of Isabelle. Over the years, the doll house was pushed to the back of the attic, hidden by cartons and odds and ends. Mice nibbled through the burlap bag wrapper. They feasted on the stairs until they got indigestion.

* * *

Hannah Clarke Stephens was cleaning out her father's attic one day. Her husband, Talbot, had gone off to fight in World War II. She'd felt useless languishing from morning sickness for three months. Now she vowed that she'd get things done. As she was sweeping out cobwebs and insect carcasses, a blue kerchief on her head, she thought about the photograph her husband had sent her that day. He was so tall and proud in his captain's uniform. Hannah had worked her way to the very back corner of the attic. She shoved over the dressmaker's dummy and an old trunk. There was an odd brown shape. Slowly she lifted some burlap that was so old the coarse cloth fell into threads. Suddenly she realized what it was. A worn white house with green shutters. Tucked inside a yellow room she saw a small paper parcel tied with string. Inside were an old dried twig and a maroon-colored sofa. She opened more packages. There were chairs and beds. On the walls of the doll house were tiny tattered curtain remnants. She picked up the doll house and moved it to the edge of the attic, then carefully carried it down the stairs. That evening when her father came home from work, she told him what she'd found.

"That was your mother's pride and joy,"
he said. "When she was pregnant with you she told me she wanted you to play with it just as she had."

"I wonder why Granny never got it out," Hannah said.

"I wonder. . . . " her father said.

* * *

A few months later, Hannah's daughter, Catherine, was born. On her eighth birthday, Catherine received the doll house. It was now red with green shutters. Hannah and Talbot had worked long nights putting flowered wallpaper in the bedrooms and painting the parlor and kitchen of the house. Talbot had figured out a way to add lights to the doll house. Hannah had found a canopy bed in a toy store and she'd recovered the old chairs. Talbot had even painted tiny pictures for the walls. Hannah had stenciled tiny pale blue rocking horses in the baby's bedroom.

Every day Hannah stood at the door listening to Catherine talk to her little dolls, combing their hair, having them get ready for the ball that evening.

* * *

The end of the century is coming soon. Hannah is looking forward to writing the year "2000" on her checks and letters. But what she's most excited about on this day is a visit from her great-granddaughter, Isabelle. Isabelle is a tiny baby in Sarah's arms. Sarah, born during the Vietnam War, is the daughter of Catherine and grandaughter of Hannah.

Already the three have made tiny books, a dictionary and a thesaurus, for the doll house, Isabelle's legacy. Hannah had the outside of the house painted a soft Victorian rose color. Sarah sewed red and white checked curtains for the kitchen. For years the three women have been combing antiques stores and toy shops for more treasures. Hannah found a pair of men's hip-boot waders, a fishing rod and a tiny creel. Catherine bought a croquet set and a bassinet and a toy box which she stuffed with a miniature jump rope, a teddy bear and a very tiny doll. The three women spend endless hours rearranging the doll house furniture.

"Wouldn't it be fun to make an entire library shelf of lilliputian editions?" Sarah asks. "We'd include *Gulliver's Travels*!"

"I've always wanted a leather chair and a standing reading lamp next to the desk," Catherine says.

"I'd like a painter's studio in the attic," Hannah says dreamily, "with a divan and an easel."

They take turns propping up Isabelle, with her red peach fuzz, next to the doll house. Isabelle, who was born in peace time. Hannah, Catherine and Sarah, each privately, are thinking of how much fun it will be to listen to Isabelle eight years from now. Isabelle will help her tiny family prepare for the ball. She'll spread out pretend picnics on the lawn next to the dusty rose house with gray shutters. Isabelle will help her family sleep and bathe and eat and read and sing and dance. No matter what happens outside, inside, a life of mystery and delight awaits. ♦

* * *

THE COLLECTION

KEN ROBBINS
Kayenta Megalith
Author and illustrator of numerous books including his most recent series *Earth, Air, Fire* and *Water,* (Henry Holt), Robbins' work is exhibited on the East End and in New York City.

MICHELLE MURPHY
Quelques Fleurs d'Original
Currently represented by the Katharina Rich Perlow Gallery in New York, Michelle Murphy resides in Greenwich Village and Amagansett with her daughters, Alexandra and Antonia, and her husband, the designer Robert Strada.

PRISCILLA BOWDEN
Nocturne in Blue and Silver; the Thames Estuary after James McNeill Whistler
A landscape painter, she was born and raised on the West End of Long Island and moved to the East End in the late 70's where she lives with her husband, writer Jeffrey Potter. On the East End she exhibits at the Elaine Benson Gallery.

IAN HORNAK
Sunset
Ian Hornak's works are in the permanent collections of the Smithsonian, the Corcoran, the Toledo and Indianapolis Museums. His work can be seen at the Katharina Rich Perlow Gallery. The LTV painting is a tiny echo of the large romantic-realist landscapes done in the late 70's.

FRANCESCO BOLOGNA
Dory
Francesco Bologna lives and maintains a studio in East Hampton. The painting titled "Dory" was executed when he was preparing a show for the benefit of the Baymen's Association at the Bologna Landi Gallery.

CYNTHIA KNOTT
Blue Nocturne
Cynthia Knott loves the wide open skies over the ocean. "When I came here in 1989 and saw that horizon line," she writes, " I knew I'd come to stay." She is a determined practitioner of *plein air* painting and is on the beach in every kind of weather to capture the many layered light of the seaside sky.

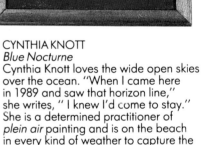

CYNTHIA KNOTT
Gold Nocturne
She has recently had solo exhibitions at the Tibor de Nagy Gallery and the Midtown Payson Galleries both in New York.

PRISCILLA BOWDEN
Fabian's Folly with Groom
after George Stubbs.
Also by Bowden and pictured elsewhere in the book are *Landscape: Perugia* after Edward Lear; *Portrait of a Young Girl* after William Holman Hunt; *The Dance* after Henri Matisse, "This dollhouse project," she says, "has raised the possibility of an interesting new career as a fine arts forger."

KATHE TANOUS
Tiny Maiden
"Largely grown in California", she made her way East in mid-life. She lives in East Hampton with her husband, advertising legend, Bob Levenson, where she paints and shows her work with Elaine Benson and others. Her work is found in homes and offices all over the world and finally, at last, in a doll house.

RYNA SEGAL
Degas *Dancer* monotype. Ryna Segal is a printmaker and teacher. "The monotype," she writes, "is a beautiful, spontaneous medium combining the best of painting and printmaking. I try to capture its rich and velvet, sensual quality."

CONNIE FOX
Sonia D's Manner
Born in Colorado, she has lived and exhibited in Albuquerque, Berkeley, Denmark, Pennsylvania and New York. Her work appears in many collections including, The Albright-Knox, Brooklyn Museum, Weatherspoon Gallery and The Parrish Museum in Southampton. Her contribution was inspired by the French painter and textile designer, Sonia Delaunay, 1885–1979.

NAN ORSHEFSKY
Big Sur
Ms. Orshefsky writes: "I was so intrigued by the problem of getting the great outdoors into a small format, I did miniature landscapes for two years after the doll house project." Her work is exhibited at Guild Hall in East Hampton, the Elaine Benson Gallery and Ashawagh Hall in Springs.

WILLIAM KING
After Brancusi, wood, 3" high
Born in Jacksonville, Florida in 1925, he was educated at the Cooper Union Art School, The Brooklyn Museum Art School and the Central School in London. His work is in all major public and private collections. He is represented by the Terry Dintenfass Gallery in New York and resides in East Hampton.

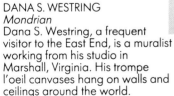

DANA S. WESTRING
Mondrian
Dana S. Westring, a frequent visitor to the East End, is a muralist working from his studio in Marshall, Virginia. His trompe l'oeil canvases hang on walls and ceilings around the world.

ARTS & CRAFTS

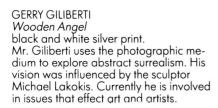

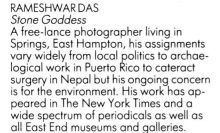

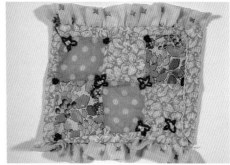

GERRY GILIBERTI
Wooden Angel
black and white silver print.
Mr. Giliberti uses the photographic medium to explore abstract surrealism. His vision was influenced by the sculptor Michael Lakokis. Currently he is involved in issues that effect art and artists.

RAMESHWAR DAS
Stone Goddess
A free-lance photographer living in Springs, East Hampton, his assignments vary widely from local politics to archaelogical work in Puerto Rico to cataract surgery in Nepal but his ongoing concern is for the environment. His work has appeared in The New York Times and a wide spectrum of periodicals as well as all East End museums and galleries.

GREG THERRIAULT
the fireplace tiles.
Greg Therriault is a professional potter who recently completed graduate studies in psychology at New York University. He works currently at Eastern Long Island Hospital and has a private practice in Sag Harbor. His pottery is exhibited in galleries throughout the East End.

PRICILLA BOWDEN POTTER
the curio cabinet.
An avid fossil collector, she makes frequent pilgrimages to Lyme Regis in England and spends her summers combing the beaches of Nova Scotia for rocks, shells and glass treasures.

ALEXANDRA LEIGH-HUNT
quilts and carpet.
Born and raised in France, she came to American at the age of 11 in 1941 because of the war. She returned to Paris in 1946 and married in 1954. She has five children and seven grandchildren and now makes her home in Sag Harbor.

ABOUT THE WRITERS

MARJORIE APPLEMAN
An award-winning playwright, her works have been produced in New York at the American Place Theater, the Circle Repertory Theater, the Manhattan Theater Club and others, as well as theaters around the country and abroad. Also a poet, her latest volume, *Against Time,* was recently published by Birnham Wood Press.

PHILIP APPLEMAN
Distinguished Professor of English at Indiana University, Philip Appleman is a renowned poet with more than 11 books published, the most recent being *Let There Be Light* (HarperCollins) and *The Voyage Home: New and Selected Poems* (University of Arkansas Press). His work has appeared in all of the major literary presses and anthologies.

FRAN CASTAN
Fran Castan's work has appeared in The New York Times, Ms., Scholastic Magazine and on WNBC and WNET and has been awarded prizes by the Poetry Society of America, New York University and the Academy of American Poets. It is anthologized by Ballantine Books, Lexington Books and Doubleday/Anchor. Her first full-length collection will be published by Canio's Editions in the spring of 1996.

SIV CEDERING
Siv Cedering lives in an enlarged doll house with her husband and their Siberian huskies, dolls, teddy bears, and pigs. She is the author of two novels, six books for children, and several collections of poetry, including *Letters From the Floating World, Selected and New Poems* (University of Pittsburgh Press). Her poem *Mother Said:* is © Siv Cedering, from *Mother Is,* Stein & Day, 1975

WILLIAM ROSSA COLE
A light verse poet, children's author, and anthologist, Cole has published over 70 books. He lives in New York and East Hampton.

B. H. FRIEDMAN
B. H. Friedman has published fiction, biography, plays and criticism. He has just completed his seventh novel, and his play "Mirrors" is scheduled for production at Guild Hall in 1996.

ERIC KRAFT
Eric Kraft has been hailed as one of America's most engaging writers. Peter Leroy, the author's alter ego, lives with his wife, the beautiful Albertine on Small's Island where he spins his stories collected in a series of novels—among them *Little Follies: The Personal History, Adventures, Experiences & Observations of Peter Leroy (so far), Herb 'n' Lorna,* and the latest, *At Home With the Glynns.* He lives in East Hampton with his wife, Madeline.

KENNETT LOVE
As a foreign correspondent for The New York Times and ABC, Kennett Love was stationed in Egypt for seven years. While there he taught journalism at the American University in Cairo.

He is the author of *SUEZ: The Twice-Fought War.* He is an avid sailor and lives in Sag Harbor.

JOE PINTAURO
Cold Hands and *State of Grace* are Pintauro's latest novels. Among his plays are: *Cacciatore, The Snow Orchid, Beside Herself, Raft of the Medusa, Men's Lives* and *Salvation.* He lives in Sag Harbor and New York City.

JEFFREY POTTER
Jeffrey Potter is the author of *To a Violent Grave: An Oral Biography of Jackson Pollock,* soon to be a motion picture with Robert DeNiro and Barbra Streisand, *Men, Money & Magic,* a biography of Dorothy Schiff, and *Disaster By Oil.* A long-time resident of East Hampton, he is the host of the television show, *Meet Your Neighbor, Neighbor* which airs on LTV.

ARTHUR PRAGER
As the director of the Irish Georgian Society, Arthur Prager has had many opportunities to study houses in the English and Irish countryside. He is a journalist and an essayist whose book *Rascals at Large or The Clue in the Old Nostalgia* captured the amazing characters that peopled the Golden Age of children's literature.

SHERIDAN SANSEGUNDO
Sheridan Sansegundo is an English-born writer who moved to the East End from Spain ten years ago. She is the arts editor of the East Hampton Star.

SILVIA TENNENBAUM
Silvia Tennenbaum is a writer who has lived in East Hampton more than half her life. She's a jack-of-all-trades but mainly a novelist, author of *Rachel the Rabbi's Wife* and *Yesterday's Streets.* She writes short stories, is a sometime journalist and art historian and is at work on an endless baseball novel and a fictionalized memoir that has frequently taken her back to Germany, where she was born in 1928.

BARBARA THOMPSON
Barbara Thompson is a writer of short stories which have appeared in many literary magazines and small presses including the *Pushcart Prize: Best of the Small Presses.* She is a regular contributor to the Writers at Work series in the Paris Review. She is also the trustee for the literary estate of Katherine Anne Porter.

LOU ANN WALKER
Lou Ann Walker is the author of *A Loss for Words* (Harper Collins), a memoir about growing up with deaf parents, which won the Christopher Award. She is also the author of several award-winning books for young readers, including *Roy Lichtenstein: The Artist at Work* (Penguin). She writes frequently for publications such as *The New York Times Magazine, The New York Times Book Review, American Photo, Parade* and others. She and her husband, author and sculptor Speed Vogel, live in Sag Harbor with their daughter, Kate.

THE MAKERS OF THE DOLL HOUSE

BUILDER: H. William Satter

It all started with granddaughters. I backed into making doll houses as a hobby when one of my granddaughters received a kit as a gift and no one else in the family wanted to put it together. Since then I have made six doll houses for granddaughters, one for a grandmother and four for charitable fund raisers—three of them for LTV. Each is more elaborate than the one preceding it, culminating in this beautiful English country house which took seven months, full time, to construct.

NEEDLEWORK: Alexandra Leigh-Hunt

If you haven't yet read The Borrowers *by Mary Norton you must. I read it to all my children and they adored the book as I did. It's all about the tiny people who secretly live in big houses and "borrow" all those things that go missing. My grandson and I spent hours and hours peering into the house while I was working on fitting the curtains and dressing the beds and we could easily imagine ourselves living in the rooms, participating in the musical soirees or sitting by the fire or opening all the packages under the Christmas tree. You might say we became "borrowers" ourselves only in reverse.*

I can remember where many of the fabrics in the house originated—for instance, the curtains in the lady's bedroom are from a silk lining in my mother's opera cloak. All the ribbons, laces and velvets come from her collection.

CURATOR: Priscilla Bowden Potter

Assembling the art collection for this doll house was a fascinating and educational experience. I learned that some artists understood and loved the idea of creating in miniature and took to it immediately; others were completely flummoxed. (Nobody was pressured.)

I learned that the most valuable tools for the job are the telephone, the color laser printer, X-acto saws, knives and mitre boxes, fast-drying paint (especially gilt), glue (but not glue guns), all kinds of sticky stuff, the Wharf Shop in Sag Harbor and our local frame shops.

I learned to use the word "adorable" frequently and without shame.

DECORATOR: Genie Chipps Henderson

Gathering together the hundreds of items that have found their way into this doll house has been like one extended treasure hunt. No shopping expedition was without delight and surprise, no small object rejected without first a critical eye towards recycling it into a doll house accessory. Thus do bottle tops become waste bins, a thimble a champagne bucket, and a dried thistle, the kitchen broom. Dozens of people contributed to this project but a most special thanks goes to my daughter, Lily, who took charge of broken toys, baby carriages and the cobwebs in the attic and my husband, Bill, who has given invaluable publishing expertise to this project.

SMALL TIME PHOTOGRAPHER
by Rameshwar Das

Peering into miniature worlds, I am Gulliver behind the lens, voyeur of the pint-size, a giant poking into a sub-sized stage set for *Alice in Wonderland.* Working, I get waves of memory of a toy soldier fort constructed in a cabinet when I was a child, hours spent in worlds of imagination and ingeniously crafted mini-objects.

However, I am child-size no longer, and the camera equipment unfortunately has not shrunk to doll house scale. I struggle to work out minute adjustments in camera angles and for ways to illuminate the exquisitely confined quarters for the photographs. The work has all the elements of lighting a life-size interior, except none of the lighting equipment fits into it. I finally solve most of the problem by bouncing lights off white umbrellas into the midget interior spaces. I acquire the beginnings of a good sunburn from working at close quarters with the halogen floods. Photographing, I find myself falling into the amazing detail of these miniatures, attention honed, focused into these tiny furnishings and playful art productions from the child-gone dreams of grown up artists.

This doll house project epitomizes the ability of the photograph to magnify, making larger than life from smaller than life, reproducing it without reference to scale, until size is irrelevant. One could be looking through a real building. The ironies of size redouble in the artwork made for these miniature chambers and halls. The artists worked to a scale where fingers, knives and brushes could not be used with accustomed skill, yet produced real work. In photographic works the art of the grown world was reduced ad infinitum to bits of film, then recreated in lilliputian prints for the doll house walls.

In doll house land our human world view, where everything is seen from the perspective of our body scale, is juggled and reshuffled into happy absurdity. And perhaps, just as we peer through microscopes at bacteria and paramecia, or as children observe glass-walled ant colonies, perhaps some larger being on the frontiers of the universe peers at us through telescopes as we view this miniature world. After all, aren't our own precious dwellings and habitations lost in the cosmic ocean of space and time, and even in the atmospheric soup and vast vegetative fur of our planet's surface? What a marvelous little memorial to our own insignificance!